Laughing Through the Storm

Laughing Through the Storm, 1st Edition

Story concept and text by © 2024 Kent Lefner
Illustrations and cover art by © Allyson Giolas

Editing, print preparation, formatting, back cover summary, cover and interior design provided by Staback Author Services.

Books may be ordered through popular, online retailers, the publisher's online store, IngramSpark, or by contacting the publisher at:

Page Turner Books, Inc.®
170 S. Green Valley Pkwy., Suite 300
Henderson, NV 89012-3145

Visit our website at www.ptbooksinc.com or contact us via email at contact@ptbooksinc.com.

Page Turner Books, Inc.® name and logo/imprint are copyright of Page Turner Books, Inc.®

HARDCOVER ISBN: 978-1-965788-09-7
PAPERBACK ISBN: 978-1-965788-10-3
EBOOK ISBN: 978-1-965788-11-0

Library of Congress Control Number: 2024952973

Printed in the United States of America.

First printing: January 2025

ATTENTION CORPORATIONS AND ORGANIZATIONS!
Most Page Turner Books, Inc.® publications are available at quantity discounts with bulk purchase for educational, business, or sales promotional use. For information, please visit www.ptbooksinc.com or http://ingramspark.com or call (702) 606-1775

Laughing Through the Storm

by

Kent Lefner & Allyson Giolas

PAGE
TURNER
BOOKS INC.

Henderson, NV, United States of America

Page Turner Books, Inc.®
Children's Literature for Ages 0 – 10

BOOKS BY EILEEN RAYE
"Backyard Secrets Lost and Found"
"A Ghastly, Ghostly Night"

BOOKS BY LEANNE E. STABACK, PH.D.
"Around the World with St. Nicholas and Friends"
(Illustrated by Marlin Montgomery)
"Baby, Let's Talk! Developing Baby's First 100 Words" Series
"The Brave Little Dreamer"
"Christopher and the Bouncing Beagle"
"Jaziel is a Big Brother"
"Kent and Leanne's Backyard Magic Show"
"Little Nurse Lauretta"
"Marc the Viking and the Wily Wolf"
(Illustrated by Allyson Giolas)
"Maria and the Magic of Guanajuato"
"Sloane the Smiling Sloth" and "Sloane the Smiling Sloth Storybook"
(Illustrated by Allyson Giolas)
"Shawn and the Lion's Roar" and "Shawn and the Lion's Roar Storybook"
(Illustrated by Allyson Giolas)
"Steven the Sea Turtle's Big Adventure"
(Illustrated by Allyson Giolas)

BOOKS BY OTHER PAGE TURNER BOOKS, INC.® AUTHORS
"From Giovanna to Joan" by Lorenzo DiBernardo
"Laughing Through the Storm" by Kent Lefner and Allyson Giolas
"Popcorn's Sweet Adventure" by Kent Lefner
"The Circus Clown(fish)" by Christopher L. Lomax
"The Feeling Gift" by Jeff Tally and Allyson Giolas
"The Snifftastic Journeys of Popcorn" Series by Kent Lefner
"Timothy Tadpole and the Secret Stone" by Jeff Tally
"Since You Went Away" by Teresa Tally and Boh Cooper

It was a dark and windy night. The storm outside gave quite a fright!

But inside, the family
settled in tight,
Ready for games by
candlelight.

"We're all gonna die!" Stephanie cried.

"Relax, Drama Queen," Kristen replied.

They fumbled and stumbled
for something to light.
Dexter barked once.
gave them a fright!

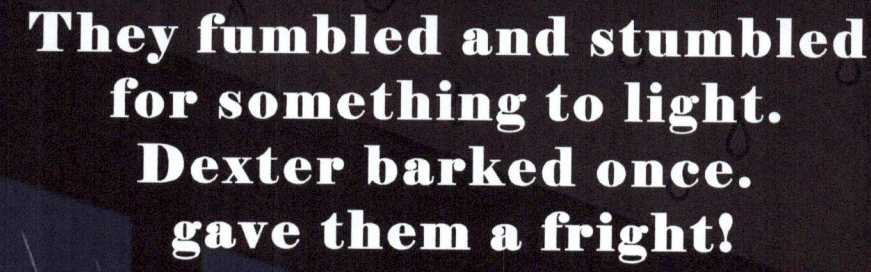

They sat on the floor
In the candlelight.
"Remember that Nerf bat?"
Mom said, with delight.

"Oh no, not that!"
Stephanie groaned.
She laughed and cried
As her eyes rolled.

"You looked like
a scientist,"
Kristen said,
"Holding that bat
right over my
head!"

Stephanie laughed,
"I didn't mean to hurt you!"
Kristen's head shook,
"I know, that i's true."

They talked of the bunk
bed and all those tricks.
Kristen kicked the top
bunk just for kicks.

"You never let me sleep!"
said Steph with a grin.
Kristen shrugged,
"It was just fun back then."

The candles flickered
as everyone laughed.
Sharing their stories
made time really pass.

The power was out
but the warmth was real.
It was the perfect
cozy family feel."

Kristen looked at Steph,
her smirk shining bright,
"You're stuck with me, kid,
day or night!"

Steph laughed,
"Like gum that won't go away!
But admit it, you'd miss
my chaos every day!'

They both burst out laughing,
shaking the floor,
Dexter wagged his tail,
ready for more.

Moving into the new house,
there was so much to do,
Boxes were everywhere
and paint buckets too.

But the best change of all
that made Kristen scream,
Was Dexter the dog—
Dad's big surprise dream!"

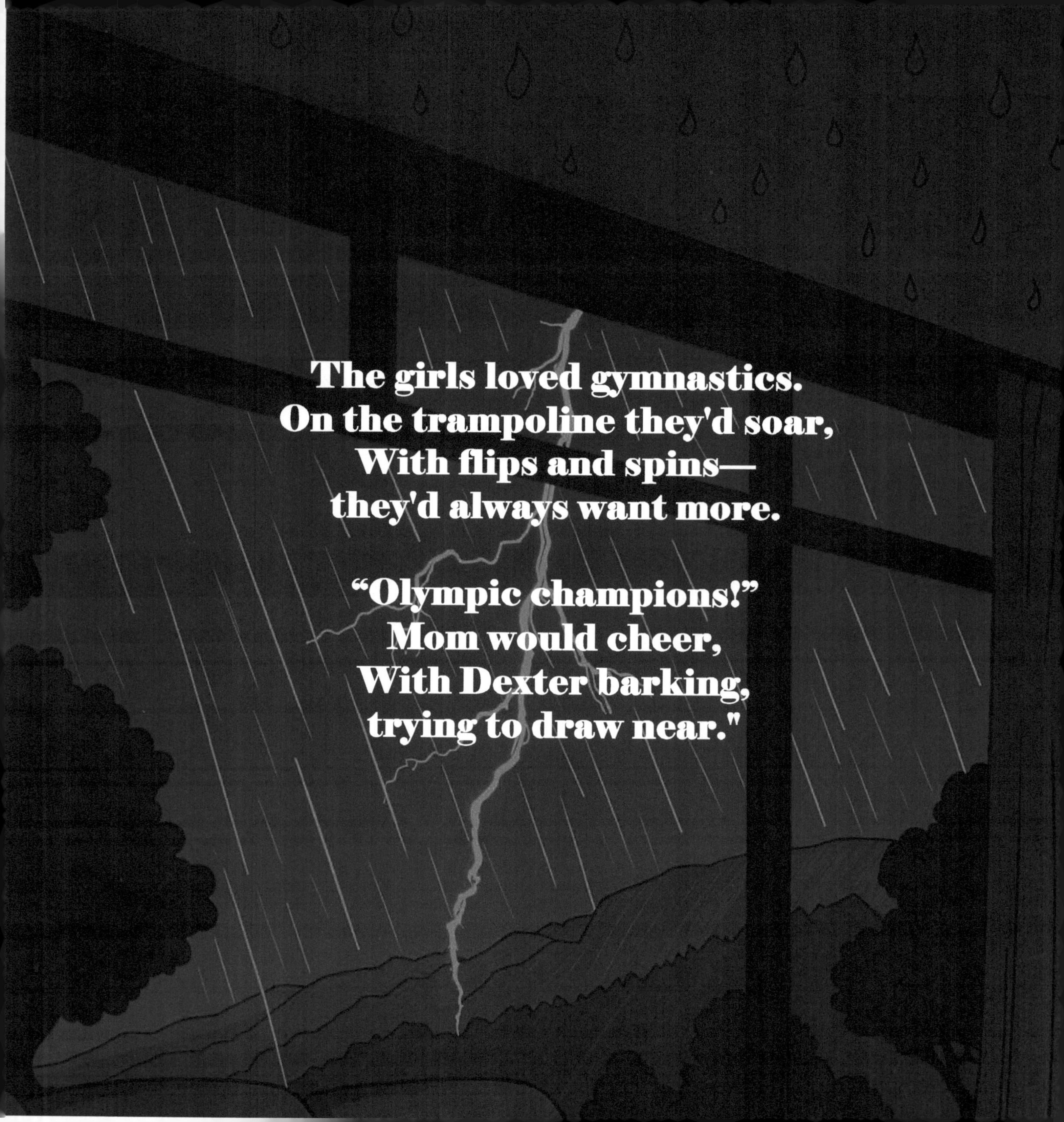

The girls loved gymnastics.
On the trampoline they'd soar,
With flips and spins—
they'd always want more.

"Olympic champions!"
Mom would cheer,
With Dexter barking,
trying to draw near."

Everyone laughed—
it was true.
Dexter loved 'helping'
with pieces too.

They all snuggled in,
waiting for light,
Enjoying the dark
that felt just right."

One day Dexter escaped, bolting out the door,
running through neighbors' yards—oh what a chore!
"Get him!" they shouted, laughter and haste.
Dexter thought it was all a fun race."

But in the end,
the new house was just right,
Trampoline flips and
dog-chasing delight.

They settled in
with family and love,
With Dexter fitting perfectly,
like a glove."

With love, laughter,
and Dexter's mischief,
Even stormy nights
become a gift.

For when a family's
together—
no matter the weather,
There's always light
when you're with each other.

About the Author

Kent Lefner

Mr. Lefner is the author of *Popcorn's Sweet Adventure*, the first book in his debut children's series, *The Snifftastic Journey's of Popcorn*; and this book, *Laughing Through the Storm*.

After a long and fulfilling career in Program Management, Kent now enjoys a quieter life in Indiana with his wife, Lisa, and their beloved dog, Popcorn.

His love for storytelling and his adventures with his family inspired this heart-warming story.

About the Illustrator

Allyson Giolas

Allyson Giolas is a Utah-based, freelance illustrator. She specializes in creating art that aims to captivate audiences through the enchanting lens of childhood.

As an artist, Allyson's motivation stems from a longing to connect with young minds.

She is committed to infusing her work with a delightful mix of creativity and nostalgia, ensuring that her art captures the world from their unique perspectives.

We hope you enjoyed *Laughing Through the Storm!* If you would like to be notified of future books in *The Snifftastic Journeys of Popcorn* series, or future publications by Kent Lefner, please let us know by emailing the publisher at contact@ptbooksinc.com.

Also, we would appreciate it if you could leave a review on the website from where you purchased this copy. Thank you!

www.ingramcontent.com/pod-product-compliance
Lightning Source LLC
Chambersburg PA
CBHW041435120626
46547CB00002B/227